Sometimes I Feel Like I Don't Have Any Friends (But Not So Much Anymore)

A Self-Esteem Book to Help Children Improve Their Social Skills

by Tracy Zimmerman and Lawrence E. Shapiro, Ph.D.
Illustrated by Timothy Parrotte

The Center for Applied Psychology, Inc.
King of Prussia, Pennsylvania

Sometimes I Feel Like I Don't Have Any Friends (But Not So Much Anymore)
By Tracy Zimmerman and Lawrence E. Shapiro, Ph.D.
Illustrated by Timothy Parrotte

Published by:
The Center for Applied Psychology, Inc.
P.O. Box 61587, King of Prussia, PA 19406 U.S.A.
Tel. (800)962-1141

The Center for Applied Psychology, Inc. is the publisher of Childswork/Childsplay, a catalog of products for mental health professionals, teachers and parents who wish to help children with their social and emotional growth.

ISBN 1-882732-58-8

INTRODUCTION

A lack of social skills is one of the most common reasons that children get referred to a counselor or therapist. In addition to the immediate problems that occur when children can't get along with others, researchers are now telling us that an inability to make friends and join a peer group may have serious long range implications as well.

This psychological storybook is designed to be read by an individual child or to stimulate group discussions. In the book, Mark finds that his inability to make friends has made him isolated and lonely. It is not so much that he doesn't have the desire to make friends, but rather he doesn't have the skills. With the help of his parents and friends Mark learns the importance of good listening, good manners, and cooperation.

This book, like the others in the Self-Esteem series, is designed to give children a role model for positive and realistic change, and to help them find new ways to cope with their problems and concerns.

Hi. My name is Mark and I'm in fourth grade. I'm pretty smart in school, but until a few months ago, I didn't have many friends. So I spent a lot of time alone.

Nobody in my class seemed to like me very much. I don't really know why, they just didn't.

Like one time we were playing kickball in gym class. The first kid that was up totally missed the ball. He looked so silly, so I said "Loser" under my breath.

Except…the kid heard me and ran to the teacher. Some of the kids said, "You're a jerk. You're the loser" but I didn't care. I just said, "I am rubber and you are glue so whatever you say bounces off me and sticks to you. So you're the jerks!"

But I had to stay after school and clean all the blackboards.

Once John and Mike were playing a board game at recess and I asked if I could play with them. They said "Sure."

But they didn't know the right rules, so I had to keep telling them how to play.

Then they started cleaning up the game right in the middle of my turn and said they had to go! They left me sitting there alone.

Things were sorta weird at home too.

My older sister Jill had lots of friends who came over after school. They rode bikes and did their homework together and sometimes they'd stay over for dinner.

They hardly ever asked me to play with them.

It seemed like no one ever wanted to be around me.

So I'd stay in my room and read my library books or play with my dog, James. James loves me and likes to lick my face.

Then one day last month, EVERYTHING went wrong and I thought that EVERYONE was against me.

My soccer team had our championship game last week against our rival school. I was totally psyched to win the trophy so I planned to play my hardest.

Someone passed me the ball and I started dribbling it down the field when two big guys from the other team ganged up on me and one of them tripped me, and the other one kicked me after I fell.

The ref didn't even call it!

I got so mad that I ran over and started screaming at the ref (which I found out you are not allowed to do).

My coach yelled at me from the sidelines to calm down, but I didn't hear what he was saying. So I ran after the two guys and tackled one of them. I was so mad!

The coach came out on the field, picked me up and carried me back to the bench.

The ref kicked me out of the game—and it was only the first quarter.

And the other kids looked at me like I was a jerk.

Usually after games, my parents took me and Jill out for pizza, but they didn't that time. They said that they were really disappointed in me. They said my behavior didn't deserve a pizza treat that night.

When we got home, I went to my room and slammed the door. I yelled "I HATE EVERYBODY!" Then I just laid on my bed and stared at the ceiling.

Later on I heard a knock at my door. It was Dad. He said he wasn't mad at me anymore and asked if I wanted to talk about what had happened earlier at the game.

I didn't say anything.

But later that night I went into my parents' room and told them I felt like I didn't have any friends, and that nobody liked me.

They said that my teacher, Mrs. Bixley, had said that I seemed unhappy at school, too, and she had some suggestions of what to do to help me make some friends.

I said I would try.

First we worked on <u>cooperation</u>. Mrs. Bixley taught me that I need to let other people have their turn and listen to what they have to say without blurting things out.

So next time somebody said something dumb in class, I just kept my mouth shut and listened.

Then we worked on <u>manners</u>. One day this kid Bob was trying to play basketball, but he was throwing the ball all wrong, and it never went in.

The "old" me would have grabbed the ball away and shown him how to do it right. But this time I just asked him if I could play, too. He said yes, and I made my first friend that day. Now Bob and I play together all the time.

Mrs. Bixley helped me make what she calls a "Social Success Chart."

Every time I do something cooperative at school, like help somebody else with a math problem or stay quiet when Mrs. Bixley is talking, I get a smiley sticker on the chart. If I get four stickers in one day, I get 15 minutes extra on the computer.

After I got so good on my Social Success Chart that I got to use the computer nearly every day, Mrs. Bixley had a talk with my parents. They all thought it would be a good idea if I joined a group of new people—kids I had stuff in common with.

Since I like to read so much, my parents found a Kids Book Club at our library. They met every Saturday and talked about stories they read during the week.

On the morning of the first club meeting, I was sorta nervous.

In a few minutes, a couple other kids showed up that looked like they knew each other. I remembered what Mrs. Bixley said about taking turns and about making eye contact with people, so I waited until they finished talking before saying "Hi." One girl seemed really nice and asked if she could sit next to me!

Mrs. Bixley told me, "Everybody likes a good listener," so I practiced listening to everybody and I let them finish before I said anything at all.

By the time the book club was over that month, I had made two new friends that didn't even go to my school. (And I got to read a whole lot of books, too.)

Bob is my best friend now, even though he's not in my book club on Saturdays. He comes over to my house and we do homework together and shoot hoops in the driveway. We take turns on whose house we visit, too.

43

I like him a lot. And I think he likes me too. My parents say I'm so much nicer to be around. I smile more now too. They said they're glad to have a happy son again.

And guess what? One day last month the teacher announced we'd be getting another new kid in our class—and she asked ME to show him around!

ABOUT THE PUBLISHER

The Center for Applied Psychology, Inc. is the country's largest distributor of psychologically-oriented products, including therapeutic games, books, videotapes, audiotapes, computer software, posters, and teachers aids. Its Childswork/Childsplay catalog is designed to help professionals, parents, and teachers address the mental health needs of children and their families through play. Featuring over 100 resources that deal with such issues as impulsivity, divorce, self-control, coping skills, classroom behavior, family problems, bereavement, self-esteem, anger control and behavior problems, the product line has been lauded as the "most complete collection of products to help children with their social and emotional concerns."

The Center also provides up-to-date and innovative training in child and adolescent psychology for psychologists, social workers, and counselors throughout the year and throughout the U.S. Professionals can earn Continuing Education (CE) credits by attending workshops on such topics as Short-term Therapy with Children, Techniques and Strategies to Help the Angry Child, Adolescent Depression, Short-Term Therapy with Oppositional/Defiant Children, and Child Sexual Abuse.

The Childswork Book Club gives its members access to the most complete collection of psychotherapeutic books for children. Book Club members have the opportunity to purchase just-published and popular books on childhood concerns from ADHD to anger control, depression to divorce, and self-esteem to social skills. Featured titles as well as self-help books, therapeutic storybooks, and professional textbooks are offered at significant savings, as are other Childswork/Childsplay products.

The Child Therapy News is published bimonthly to offer mental health professionals the most complete source of information about a specific childhood disorder or issue. Each issue includes a full-length article detailing the most pertinent and up-to-date information of the subject, an in-depth interview with an expert, and a profile on a model treatment program. Past issues have addressed ADHD, anxiety disorders, sexual abuse, oppositional/defiant children, autism, gender identity disorders, child custody, and more.

For more information on the Childswork/Childsplay catalog, professional training, The Childswork Book Club, and/or The Child Therapy News, call 800/962-1141 or write The Center for Applied Psychology, Inc., P.O. Box 61587, King of Prussia, PA 19406.